COUNTRIES

Poland

Ruth Thomson

PowerKiDS
press™
New York

Published in 2011 by The Rosen Publishing Group Inc.
29 East 21st Street, New York, NY 10010

First Edition

Editor: Steve White-Thomson
Designer: Amy Sparks
Picture Researchers: Ruth Thomson/
    Steve White-Thomson
Series Consultant: Kate Ruttle
Design Concept: Paul Cherrill

Library of Congress Cataloging-in-Publication Data

Thomson, Ruth, 1949-
Poland / by Ruth Thomson. -- 1st ed.
    p. cm. -- (Countries)
Includes index.
ISBN 978-1-4488-3277-4 (library binding)
1. Poland--Juvenile literature. I. Title.
DK4147.T47 2011
943.8--dc22

                    2010023714

Photographs:
Alamy: Paul Thompson Images front cover; Dreamstime:
Sebastian Czapnik 11, Artur Ebrowski 18; Neil Thomson
23; Photolibrary: Frank Fell/The Travel Library 5, Egmont
Strigl 14, Henryk T. Kaiser 15, 16; Shutterstock: puchan 1/19,
Wiktor Bubniak 2/8, Kapa1966 6, Nightman1965 7, Tomasz
Niewęglowski 9, Agata Dorobek 10, Wojciech Kozlowski
12, Marcin Niemiec 13, stormur 17tr, Elzbieta Sekowska
17tl, Krzysztof Slusarczyk 17br, Jaroslaw Grudzinski 17bl,
ann&chris 20, EVRON 21.

Manufactured in China
CPSIA Compliance Information: Batch #WAW1102PK: For Further Information
contact Rosen Publishing, New York, New York at 1-800-237-9932

Web Sites

Due to the changing nature of Internet
links, PowerKids Press has developed
an online list of Web sites related to
the subject of this book. This site is
updated regularly. Please use this link
to access this list:
http://www.powerkidslinks.com/cou/poland

Contents

Where Is Poland?

Here is a map of Poland. It is a
large country in Eastern Europe.

4

Warsaw is the capital city.
It is the biggest city in Poland.
The Vistula River flows through it.

Buildings in Warsaw town square were rebuilt after they were destroyed in World War II.

Land and Sea

Land in central Poland is flat. Hills and mountains stretch across the south. There are lakes and forests in the north.

There are more than 1,000 lakes in Poland.

Pine trees cover the lower slopes of the mountains.

Along the north of Poland is the
Baltic Sea. The beaches are wide
and sandy. Huge ships and ferries
dock at several ports.

Tugboats pull big ships into port.

The Weather

Poland has mild springs and warm summers. Sometimes there is heavy rain.

In the summer, many people take trips to the mountains to walk and climb.

It is cold in the winter. In the mountains, there is deep snow and cold frosts.

You must dress in warm clothes when you go out in the snow.

9

Town and Country

Towns have a market square in the center, often with colorful old buildings. There are more modern buildings on the edge of towns.

Town squares are often closed to traffic.

10

There are many small farms in the country. Farmers mainly grow rye, potatoes, and cabbages.

Poland is famous for its organic vegetables.

Some small farms still use horses to pull farm machines.

Homes

In cities, there are many old housing complexes with rows of tall apartment buildings. More colorful modern apartments have green spaces, paths, and stores nearby.

These apartments have balconies where people can sit in good weather.

In the country, many old
houses are built of wood.
These are usually one-story
high. Some have thatched roofs.

The people in this
house keep bees in
the straw beehive.

Shopping

People shop for food in huge markets, supermarkets, and small, local stores and shops.

People can buy canned food and drinks in markets, as well as fruit and vegetables.

There are new shopping centers on the edges of cities. People shop here for clothes and household goods, such as pans and bed linen.

Shopping centers stay open late, so people can visit them after work.

GALERIA KRAKOWSKA

GALERIA KRAKOWSKA

SATURN

 Food

Families eat their main meal together when everyone comes home from school and work.

Pork is roasted or made into ham or sausages.

People buy bread, hot dogs, and other snacks from street stalls.

16

The most popular food in Poland is pork. Here are some of Poland's favorite foods.

borscht
(cold beetroot soup)

pirogi
(stuffed dumplings)

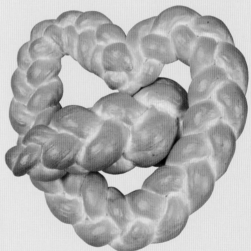

braided bread

pork

Sports

Soccer, swimming, and horseback riding are popular sports in Poland. People ride quad bikes along special tracks through forests and marshes.

Bends and humps in the tracks make quad biking exciting.

People canoe and kayak on the many lakes and rivers. In the winter, they ski on the snowy mountain slopes.

Canoeists can paddle from one lake to another through canals.

Holidays and Festivals

Most Polish people are Roman Catholics. Many go to church on Sundays. Christmas and Easter are important religious holidays.

At Easter, people paint or scratch patterns on the shells of hard-boiled eggs.

In the summer, there are folk festivals.
People wear colorful costumes and
parade through the streets. Dancers
perform to violin and accordion music.

All the costumes are
decorated with embroidery.

Speak Polish!

Cześć (*ch-ay-esch*)   Hello

Do widzenia (*do vee-dzeh-ya*)   Goodbye

Proszę (*pro-sheh*)   Please

Dziękuję (*jen-koo-yek*)   Thank you

Tak (*tak*)   Yes

Nie (*n-yeh*)   No

Nazywam się… (*naz-i-vam sheh*)   My name is…

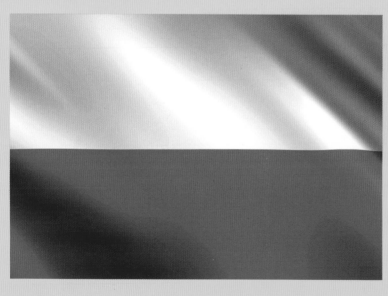

Red and white have been Poland's traditional colors for hundreds of years. White means peace. Red means bravery and strength.

Make a Polish Paper Cut

You Will Need:
- small piece of colored paper
- scissors

In the past, Polish women made paper cuts to decorate their homes. They glued these onto the walls, windows, and furniture.

1. Fold the piece of paper in half.

fold

2. Cut a shape along the unfolded edge, through both layers of paper.

3. Cut little snips on all sides of your shape.

4. Open out your finished paper cut.

Glossary and Further Information

accordion a musical instrument with a small keyboard and a folding box that you squeeze in and out to play

capital the city in a country where the government is

embroidery patterned stitching with colorful threads

folk festival an event that shows off the music, dance, and costumes of a country

housing complex a large area with lots of houses or apartments on it

Roman Catholic a Christian whose spiritual leader is the Pope in Rome

thatched covered with straw or reeds as a roof

Books

A Visit to Poland
by Victoria Parker
(Heinemann Library, 2008)

Country Explorers: Poland
by Sean McCollum
(Lerner Publications, 2009)

Let's Visit Poland
by Susie Brooks
(PowerKids Press, 2009)

Index